johnny
get inside

Favored NationS
ENTERTAINMENT

www.johnnya.com

Transcribed by HEMME LUTTJEBOER

Special Thanks to Tomo Fujita

Project Manager: AARON STANG
Music Editor: COLGAN BRYAN
Photos by PAUL LYDEN, courtesy of Favored Nations.
Production Coordinator: SHERYL ROSE
Book Art Layout: ERNESTO EBANKS
Album Artwork: © 2004 Favored Nations LLC

Johnny A. is a registered trademark.

it's sometime monday night...

A destination within sight of Boston's crown of radiant spires. Over the river and through some woods. In a tiny alleyway, an elderly two-story wooden house woven inside a busy riot of commerce and America's first college. Hidden well, you'd have to know this path was there or you'd never find the place.

Walk up to the guy with the clipboard standing watch. Pay the man, get the design of the night stamped on your wrist, bound up the steps. Inside, the streetlife vanishes behind. It's canned blues music, clinking glasses, the hum of conversation. Thread through the restaurant and up more creaky stairs to another sentinel, a wave of passage. Finally step through to the loft's inner sanctum black-light glow.

Students chatter around the bar but there's space ahead where the early birds sit in their clique at a clutch of tables up front, smoking and drinking. Faces gaze down from the ceiling—plaques of blues and R&B legends from Robert Johnson and Big Bill Broonzy, Bobby Blue Bland and Eric Clapton. Paintings asplash in voodoo color command the walls. Tradition didn't begin in this attic, but it's in full display.

In the purple half-light a drummer and bassist adjust and fuss. No fanfare announces the guitarist, but warm applause welcomes him to his perch stage right. He arranges himself on the stool where he'll spend the night. Sleepily, he plucks one of the waiting instruments from its stand, cradling it. Incense is lit, blue smoke caught rising through the brightening light as the set unfolds. And magically, the guitar awakens the player.

Colors blaze forth, the crowd sways in the flowing vibe. A warmth of tone, the birth of cool, lilting and gentle, insistent and fiery. Wide-open vistas on a postage stamp stage. Worlds of music colliding and concurring—Chet Atkins and Jeff Beck, Wes Montgomery and Scotty Moore, Clarence Gatemouth Brown and Mark

Knopfler... Jimi. It's the House of Blues, Harvard Square, Cambridge, Massachusetts. Johnny A. is onstage. And now it's sometime Tuesday morning.

Out of the blue and (almost) in the black, that's Johnny A.'s story. After pulling stints with various Boston bands, including his own, the guitar player decided to abandon the constraints of one style or image and present all styles, no pretense—an album of music for his personal enjoyment, his own artful dodge. And so *Sometime Tuesday Morning* appeared in 1999, a palette of musical hues likely to remain a snapshot in Johnny's own personal catalogue, experienced and perhaps enjoyed by a handful of friends and fellow players. But it didn't work out that way.

Johnny sold the instrumental album out of his car trunk after gigs and soon realized that the cardboard boxes of CDs didn't sit very long next to his car jack and spare. With some radio play in the New England area under its belt, *Sometime Tuesday Morning* began to grow legs. Soon a website, selling online, a national distribution deal, national airplay, tours to support the album, promotional appearances, no sleep till...whenever, wherever. A hit without hype, a fast track by accident, a career for all the right reasons.

During the four years of serving the business, Johnny burned to reclaim the studio, any studio. Not to prove to you that he could write another hit, but to remind himself that he could make music exactly as he wanted to, just like the last time. But why hurry such an unexpected and delightful career turn?

Finally the workload eased, the waiting ended and the studio time was booked. The guitars came out of their roadcases and once again they magically awakened the player. Now it's time to *Get Inside*.

This album is different. And how could it not be after a few years on the road, a change in the band lineup and Johnny's desire to push his own envelope. Oh, the same casual disregard for styles is still there, but these original compositions venture even deeper into the moods that each conjures.

As before, the guitarist has chosen to add some personal favorites—the gorgeous warmth of melody in Johnny Rivers' 1966 hit "Poor Side of Town" to a vast reworking of "The Wind Cries Mary." Like Hendrix, who also let caution and convention fly when he offered his transfigured tribute to Dylan's "All Along the Watchtower," Johnny applies his own muse to a master's tempo and texture. Disassembly required, but batteries provided.

Get Inside bops the blues, flirts with Miles, floats like a butterfly, stings like a bee. It's more aggressive, yet light and airy in places, a cool tension. It goes everywhere, anywhere. It refuses no influence, yet distills its own confluence. There are horns and (orchestra) bells, but no whistles. Smoke, but no mirrors. And, Oh Yeah, there's some great pickin' in there too! It's the product of a guitar player hanging onto his instrument for all its worth and letting it sing.

it's another morning. get inside.

—Carter Alan

contents

HIP BONE

By JOHNNY A.

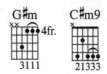

Hip Bone - 9 - 1
PGM0412

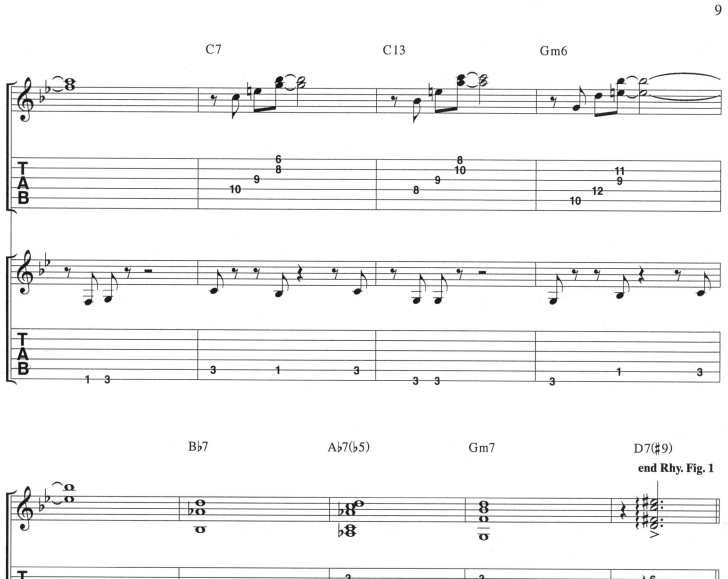

w/Rhy. Figs. 1 *(Elec. Gtr. 1)* **& 1A** *(Elec. Gtr. 2) simile*

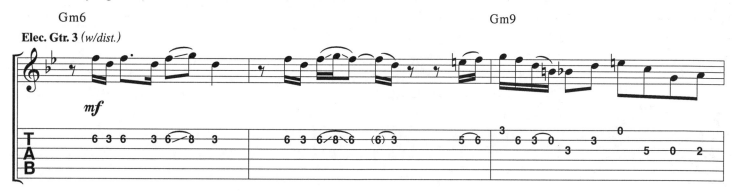

Hip Bone - 9 - 6
PGM0412

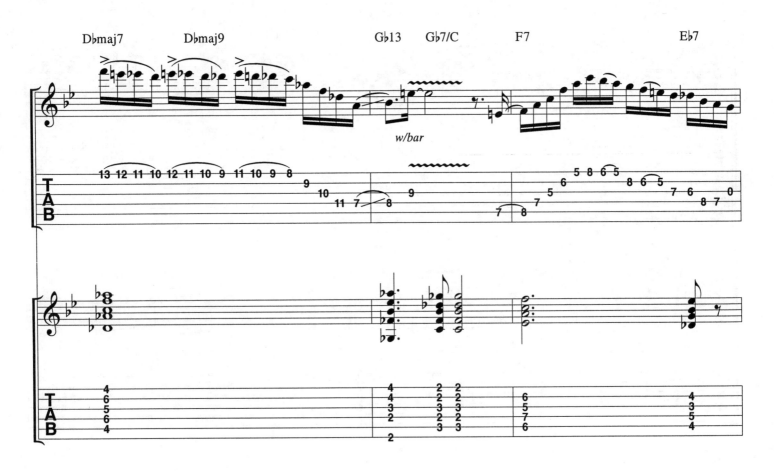

Cont. rhy. simile

C#9

G#m

Outro:

B7

C#7

hold -

*Elec. Gtrs. 1 & 2

*2 gtrs. arr. for 1 gtr.

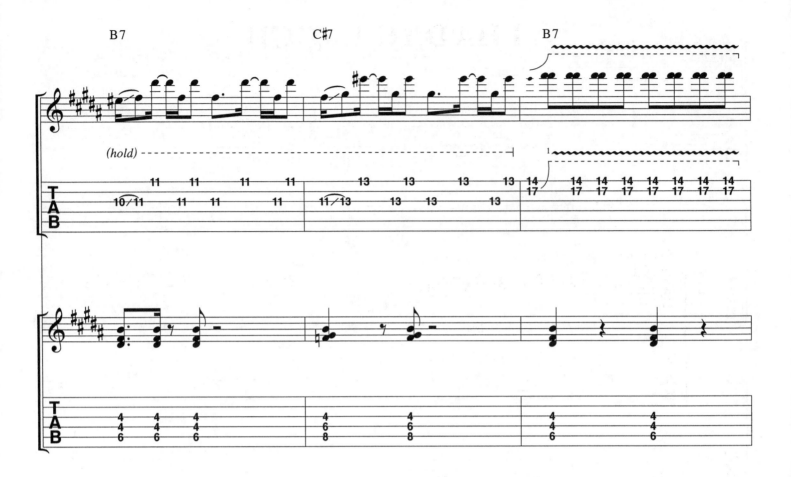

Fade

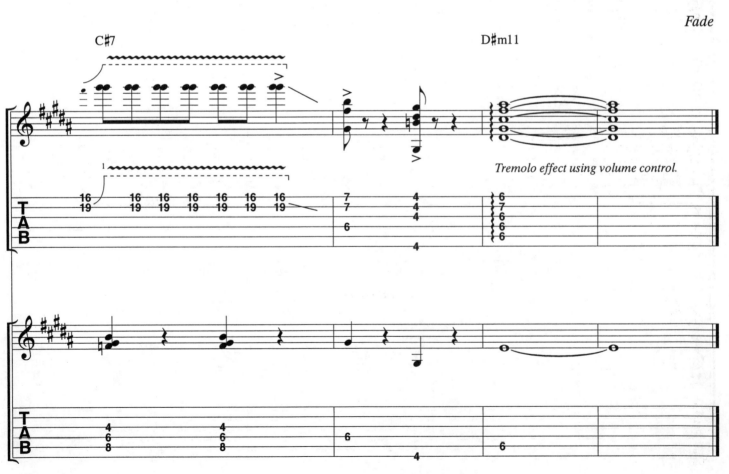

Tremolo effect using volume control.

I HAD TO LAUGH

By JOHNNY A.

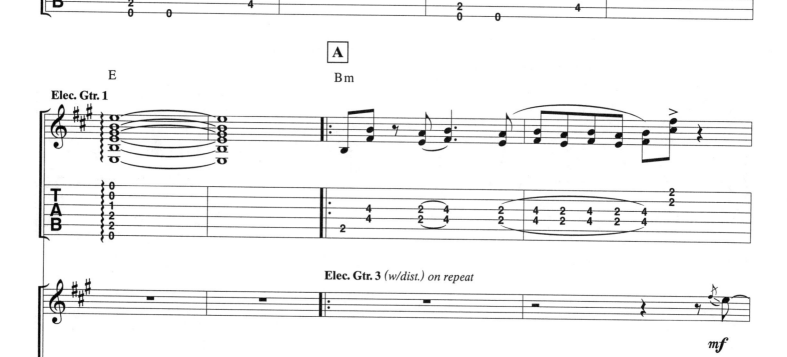

I Had to Laugh - 9 - 1
PGM0412

18

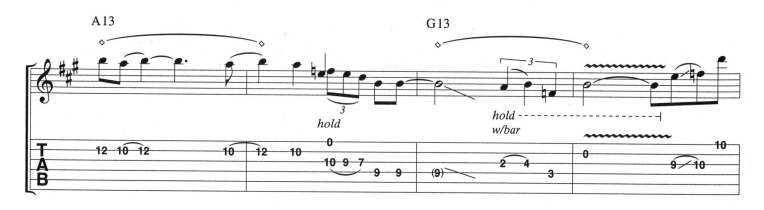

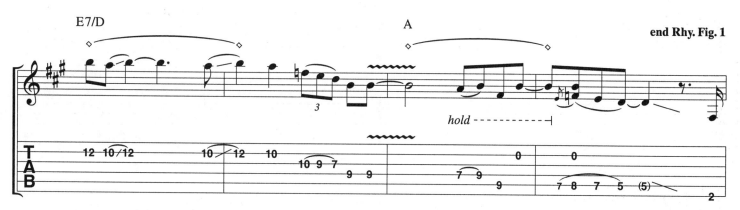

w/Rhy. Fig. 1 (*Elec. Gtr. 1*) *3 times, simile*

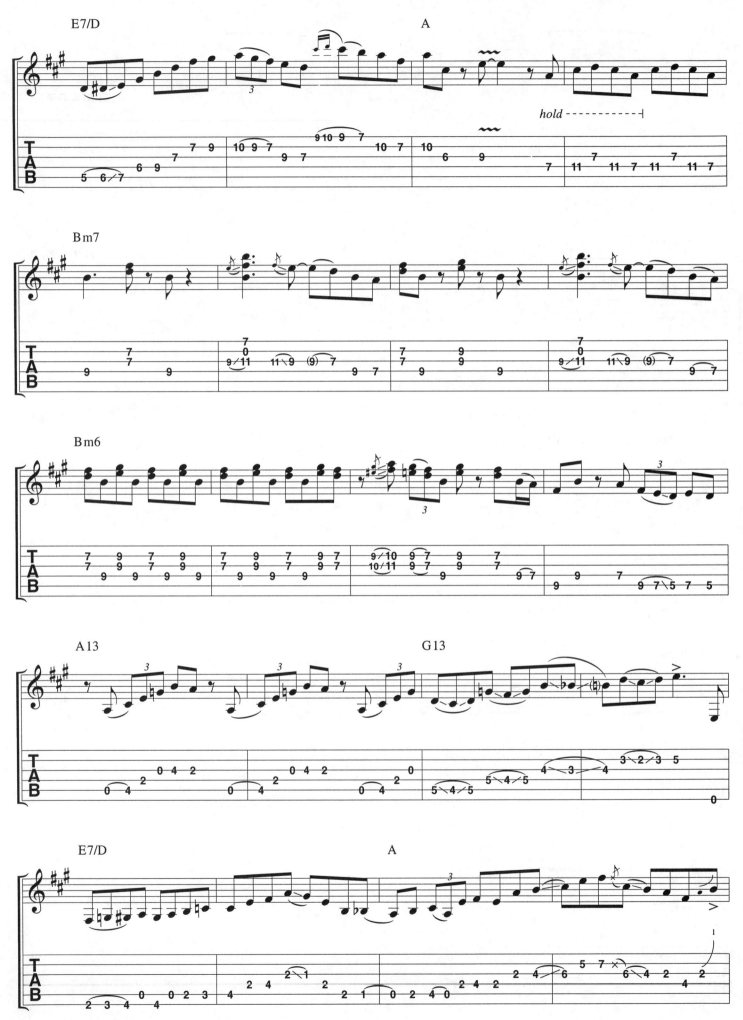

22

Outro:

I Had to Laugh - 9 - 8
PGM0412

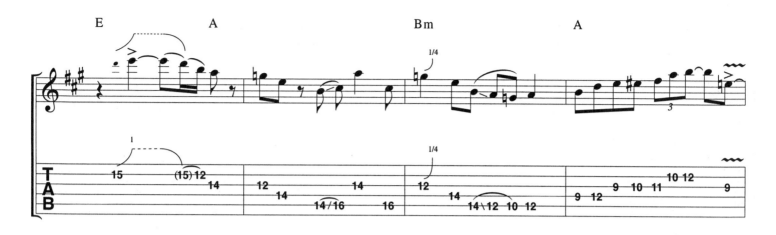

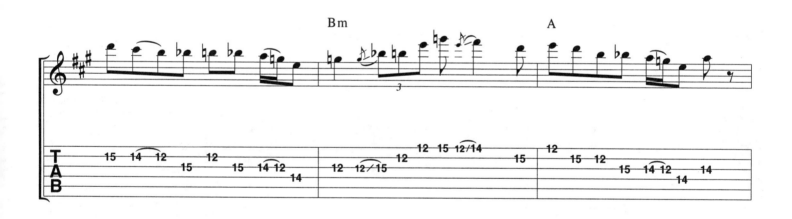

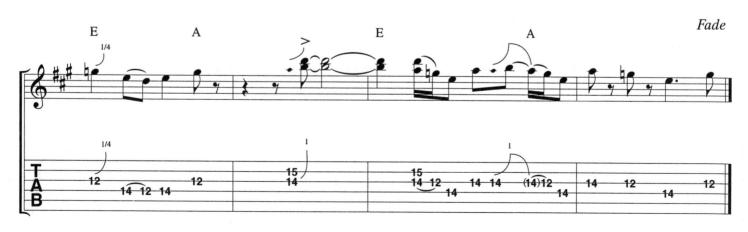

I Had to Laugh - 9 - 9
PGM0412

POOR SIDE OF TOWN

Words and Music by
JOHNNY RIVERS and LOU ADLER

Poor Side of Town - 6 - 4
PGM0412

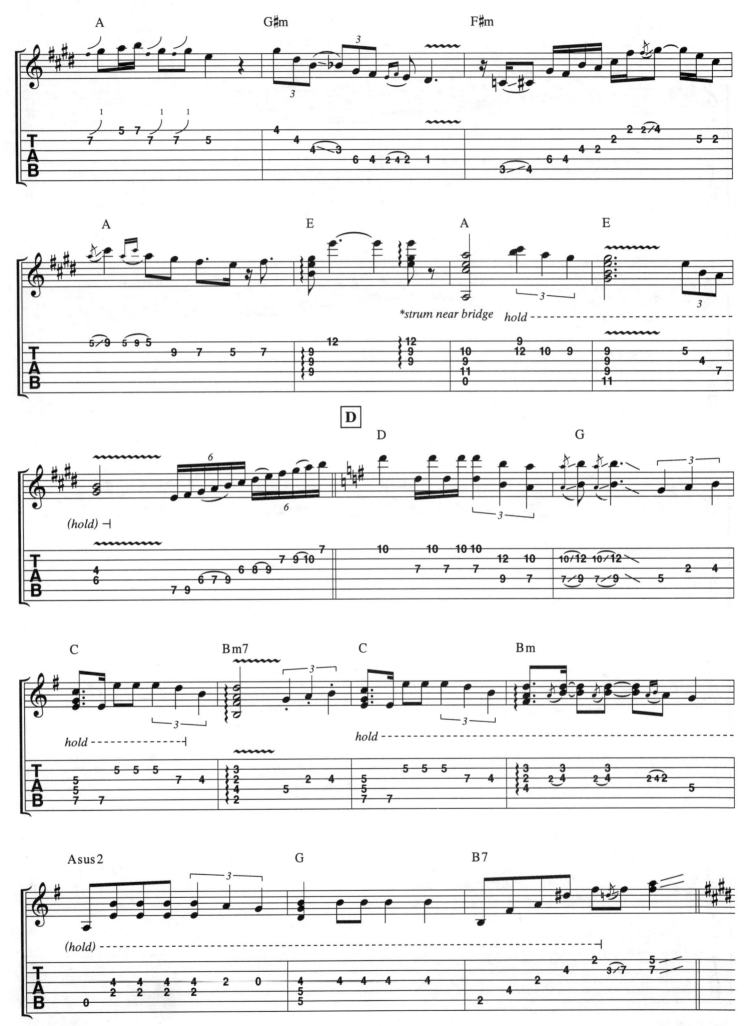

SING SINGIN'

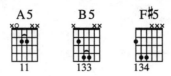

By JOHNNY A.

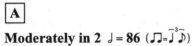

Moderately in 2 ♩ = 86

Elec. Gtrs. 1 & 2 *(w/dist.)* on repeat

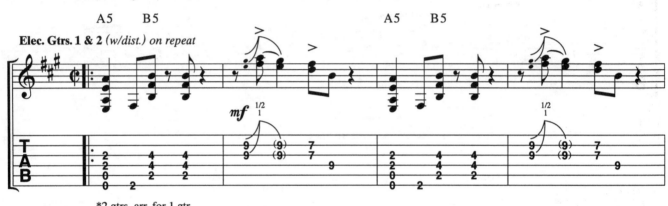

*2 gtrs. arr. for 1 gtr.

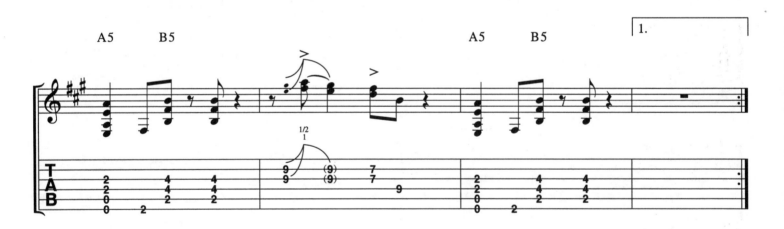

Elec. Gtr. 3 *(clean-tone)*

Sing Singin' - 7 - 1
PGM0412

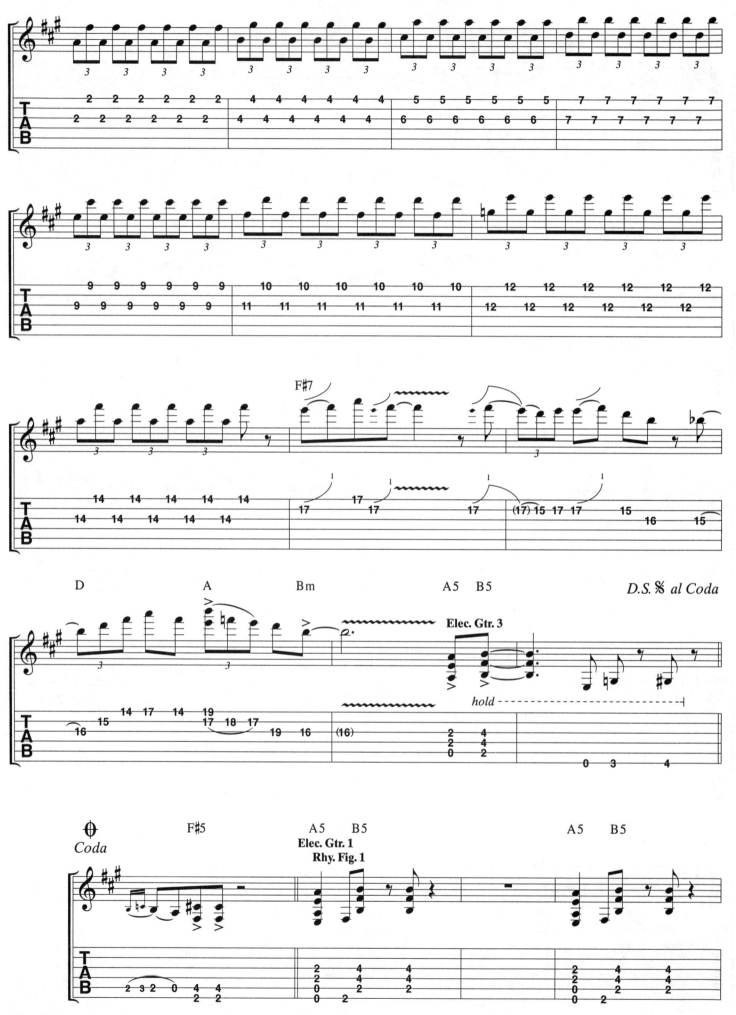

36

GET INSIDE

By JOHNNY A.

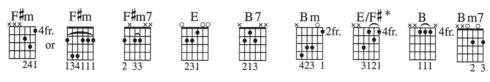

* F♯ played by bass gtr.

Moderately ♩ = 90

Intro:

*F♯ played by bass gtr.

Get Inside - 14 - 1
PGM0412

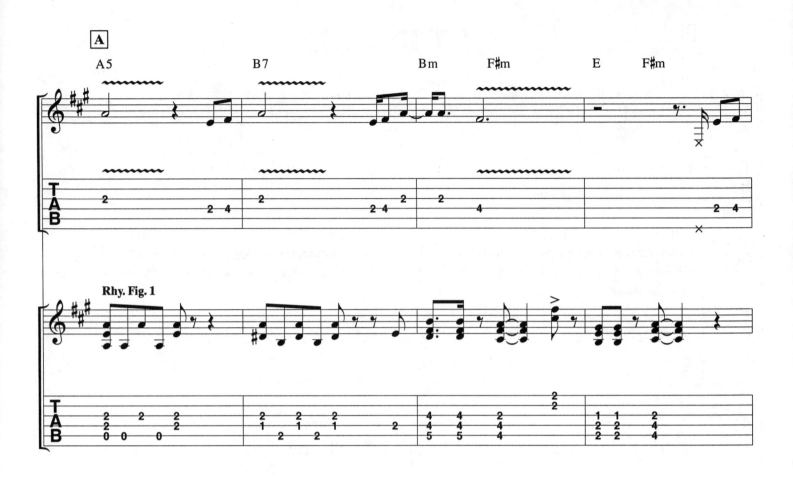

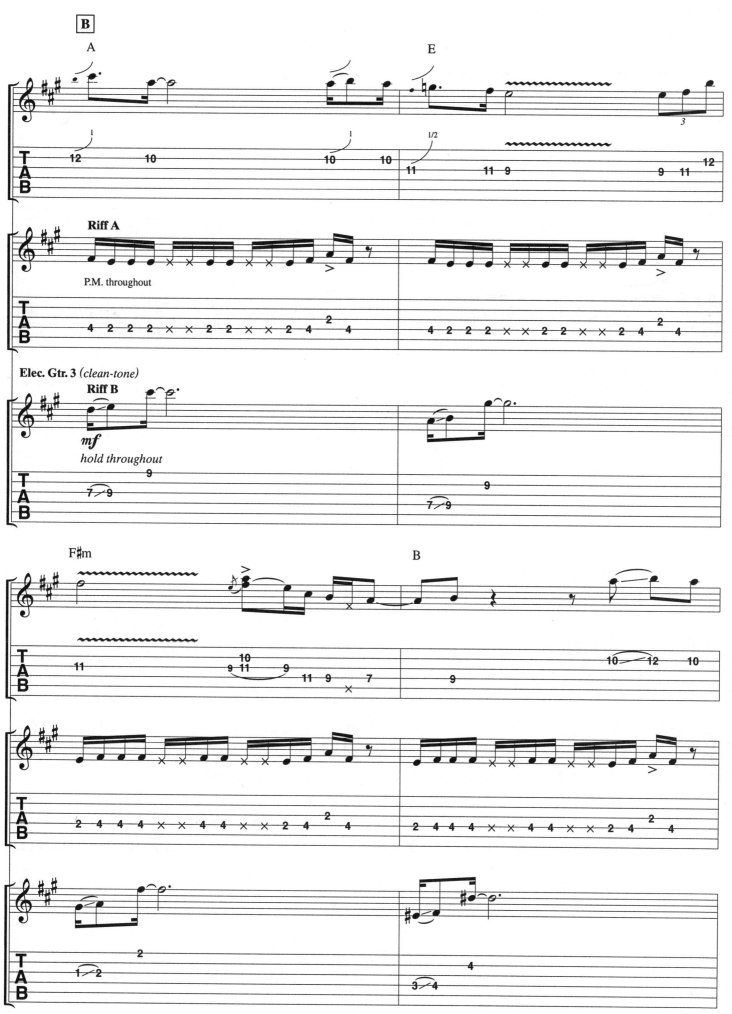

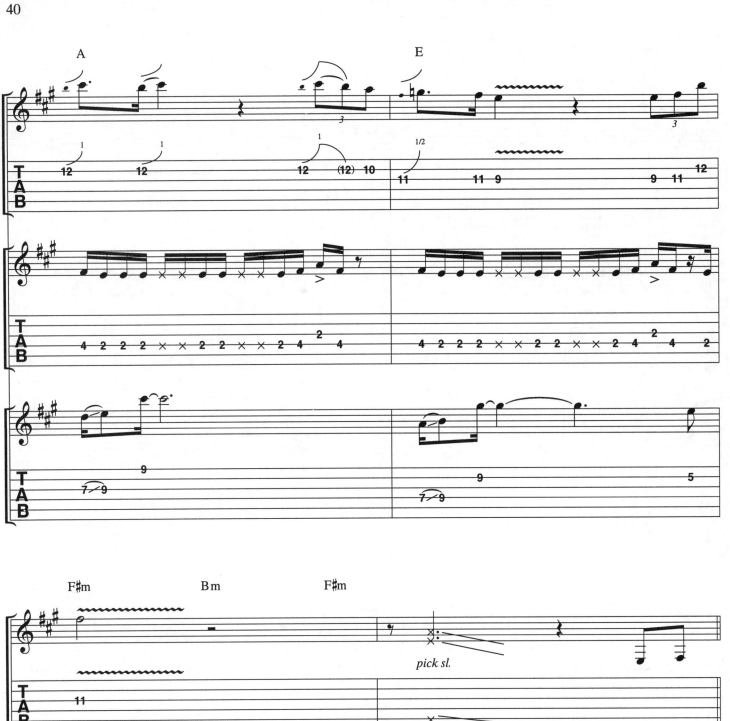

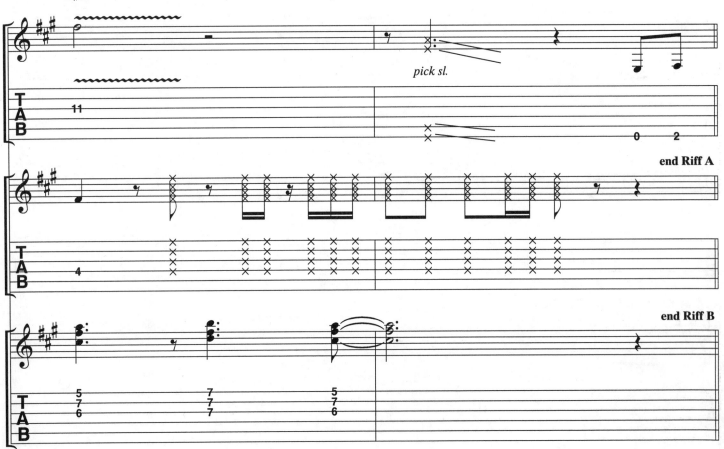

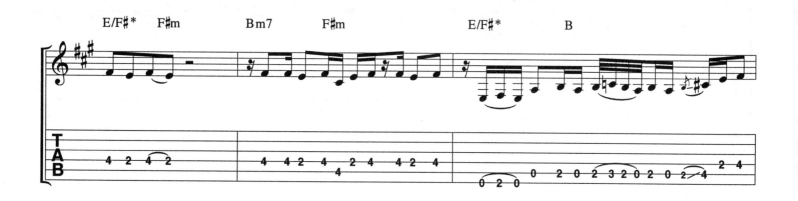

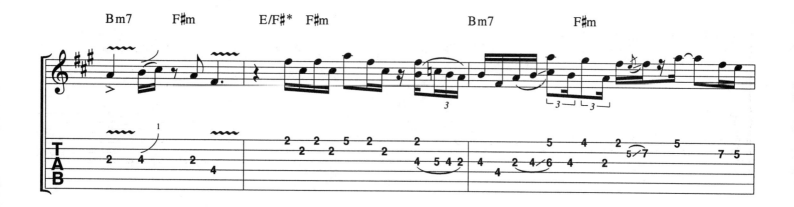

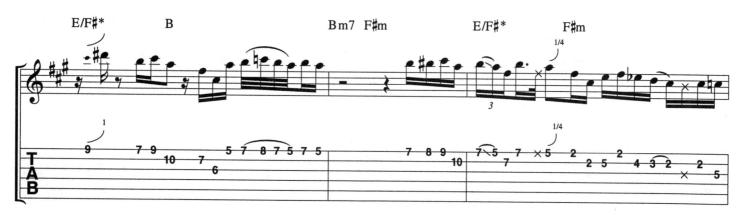

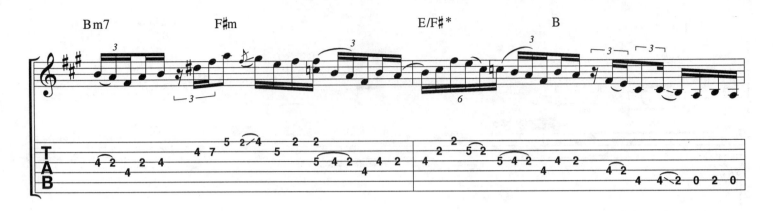

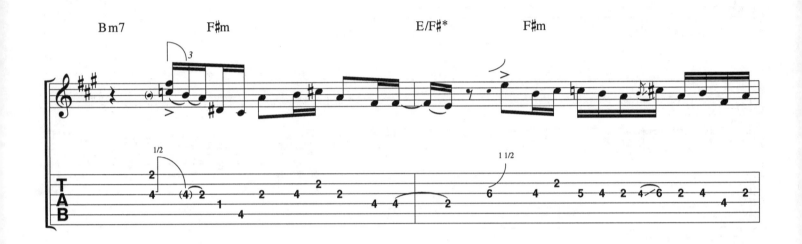

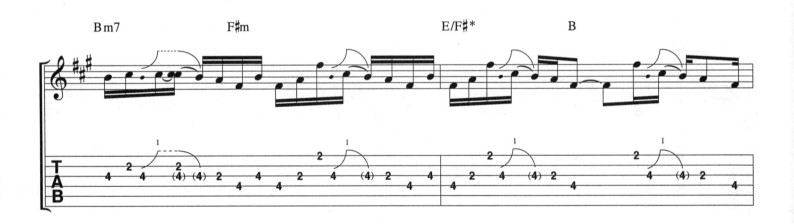

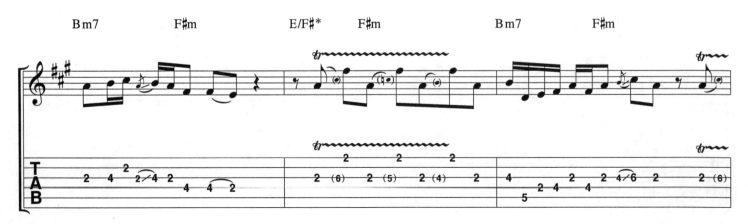

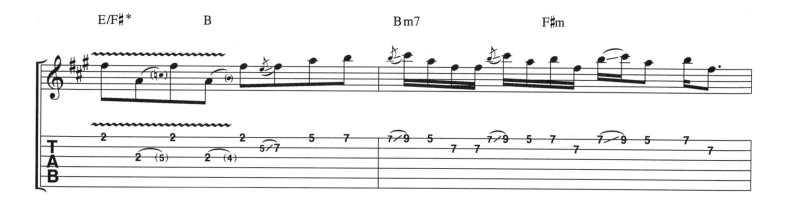

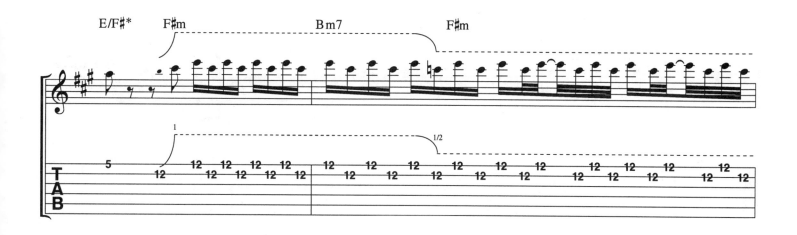

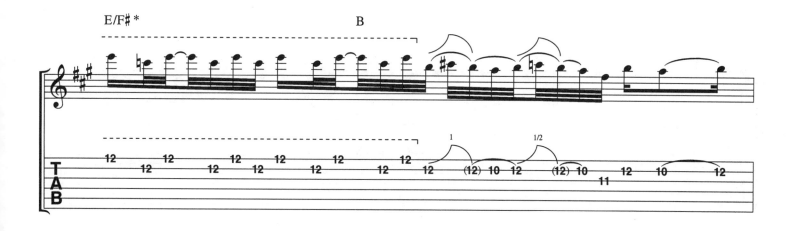

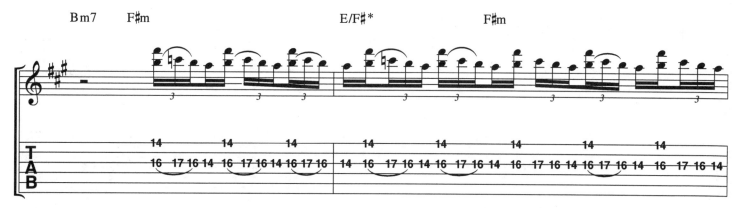

Get Inside - 14 - 13
PGM0412

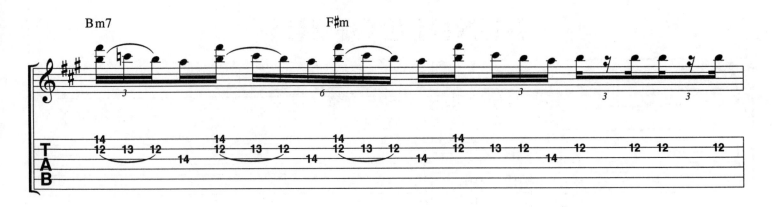

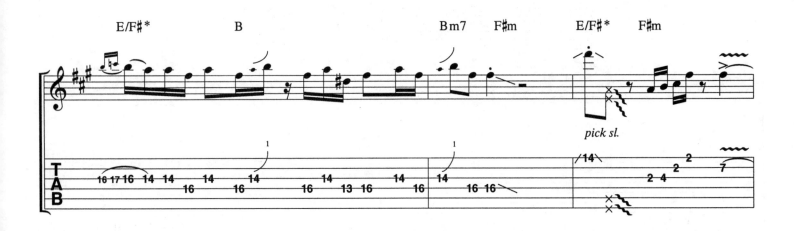

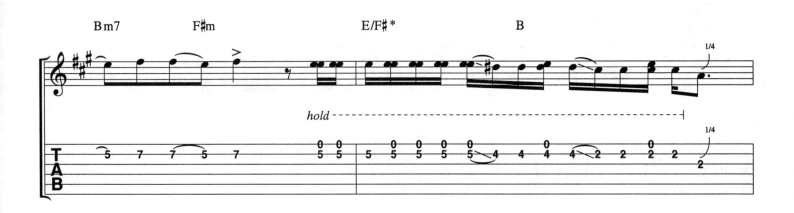

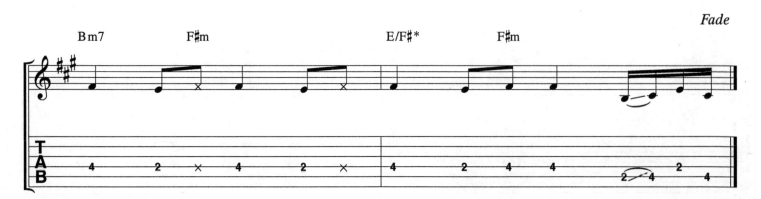

BUNDLE OF JOY

By JOHNNY A.

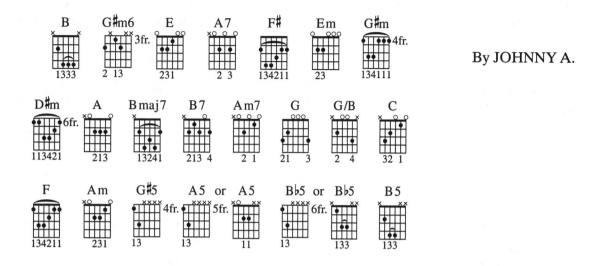

Moderate country swing in 2 ♩ = 106
Intro:

Bundle of Joy - 9 - 1
PGM0412

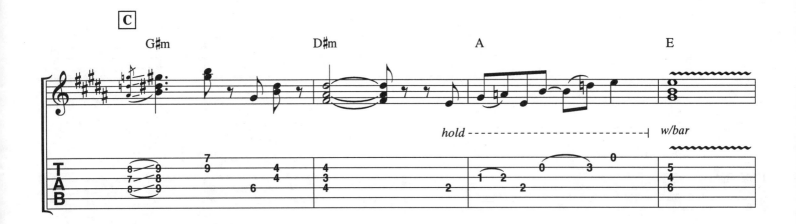

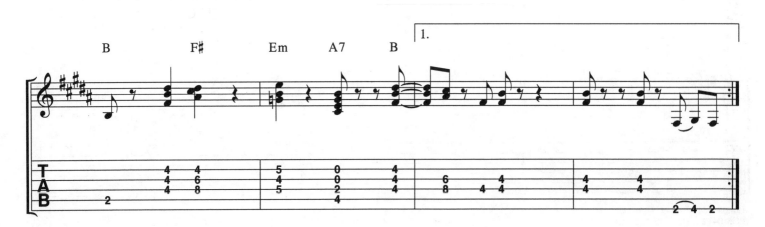

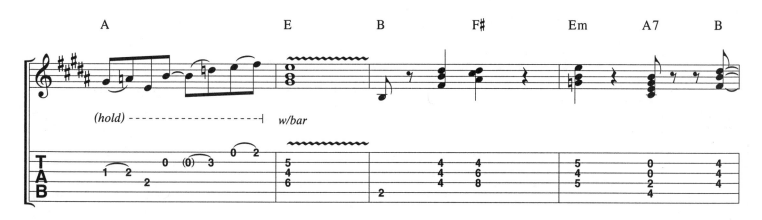

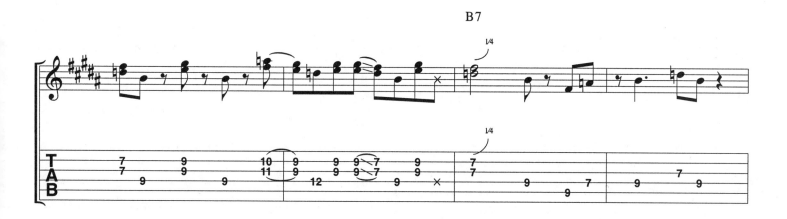

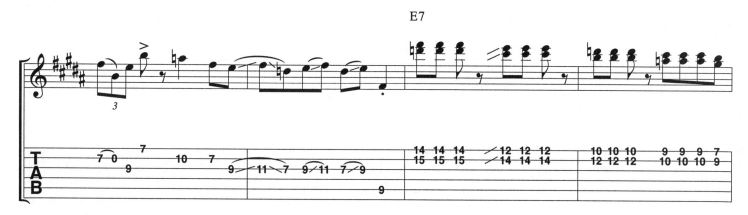

58

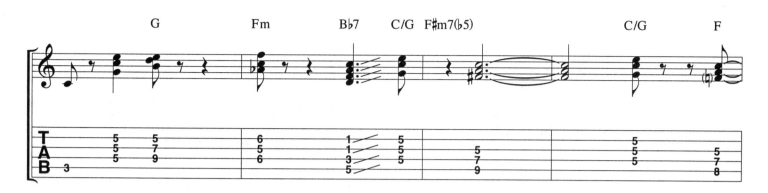

Outro:

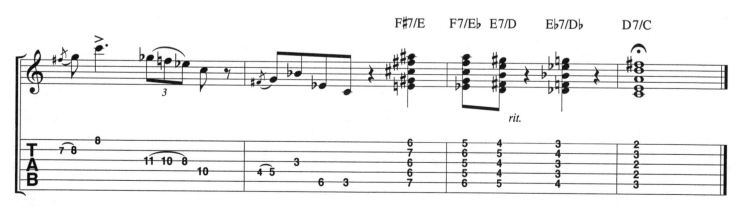

KREA GATA

By JOHNNY A.

62

63

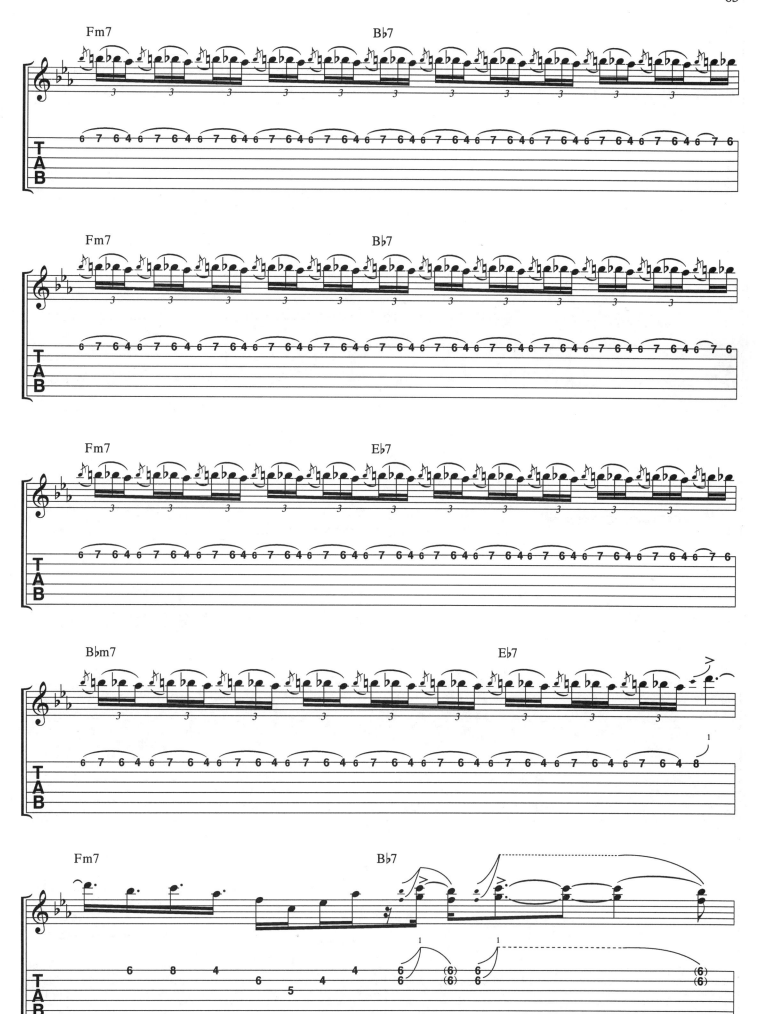

THE WIND CRIES MARY

Words and Music by
JIMI HENDRIX

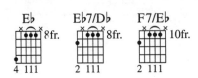

Moderately ♩ = 104

Intro:

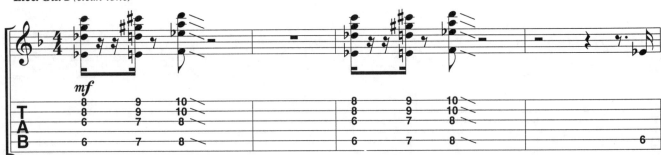

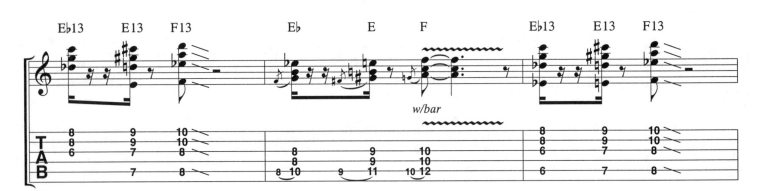

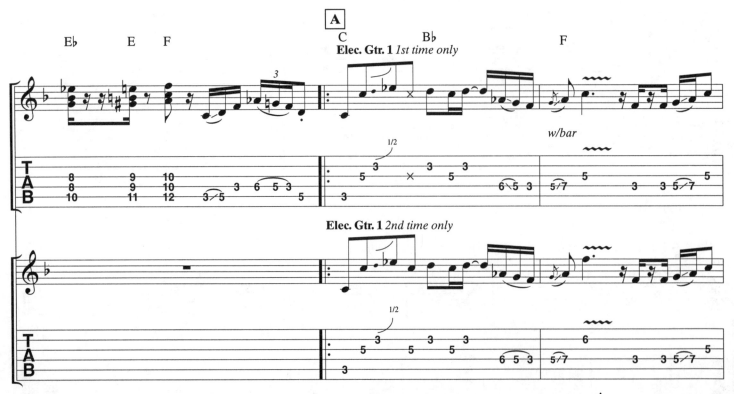

The Wind Cries Mary - 7 - 2
PGM0412

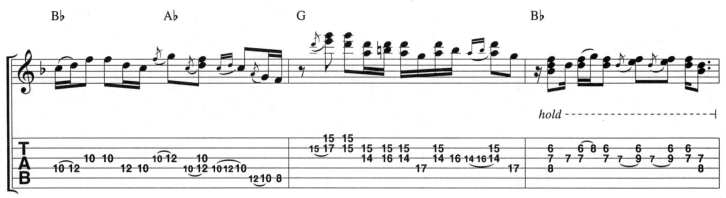

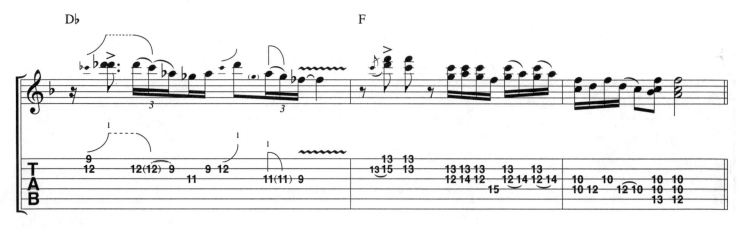

71

The Wind Cries Mary - 7 - 4
PGM0412

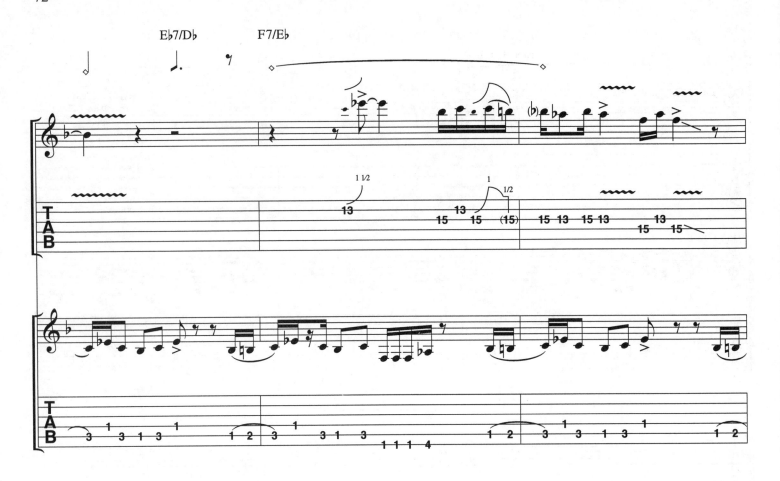

The Wind Cries Mary - 7 - 6
PGM0412

The Wind Cries Mary - 7 - 7
PGM0412

IGNORANCE IS BLISS

By JOHNNY A.

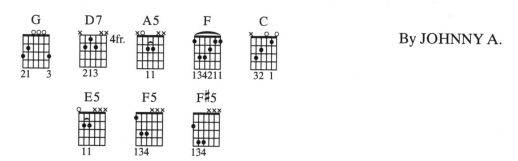

Moderately in 2 ♩ = 106
Intro:

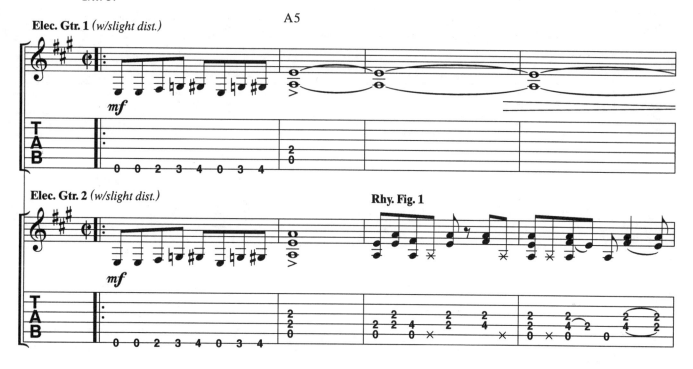

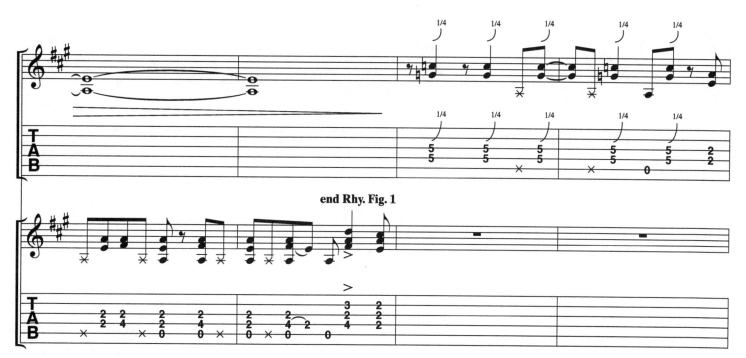

Ignorance Is Bliss - 12 - 1
PGM0412

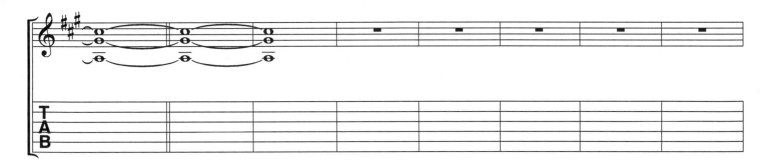

Elec. Gtr. 3   **Rhy. Fig. 4**   **end Rhy. Fig. 4**

Outro:
w/Rhy. Fig. 1 *(Elec. Gtr. 2) 7 times, simile*
w/Rhy. Fig. 4 *(Elec. Gtr. 3) 7 times, simile*

Elec. Gtr. 1

86

Ignorance Is Bliss - 12 - 12
PGM0412

SWAY A LITTLE

By JOHNNY A.

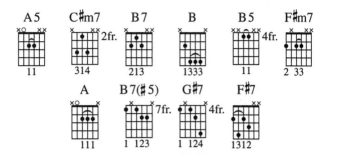

Moderately ♩ = 118

Intro:

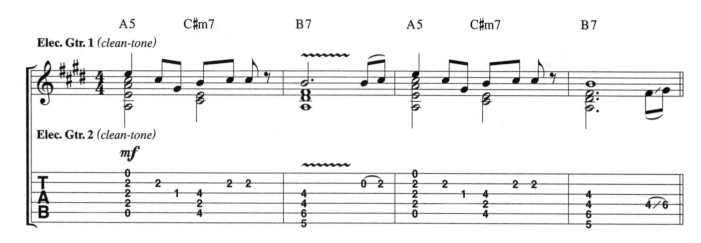

Sway a Little - 17 - 1
PGM0412

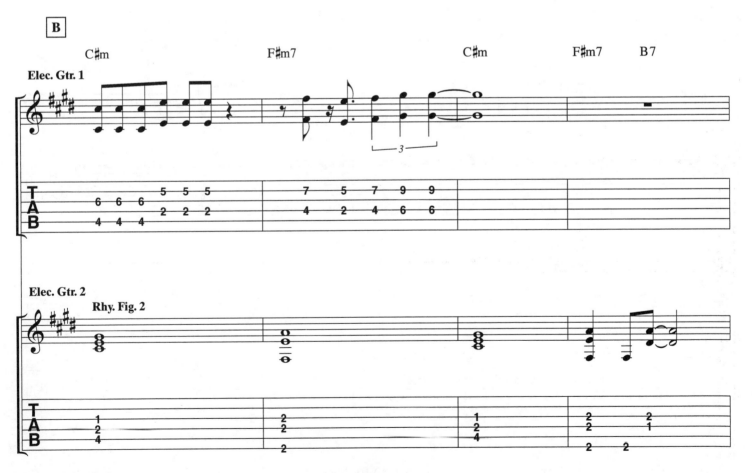

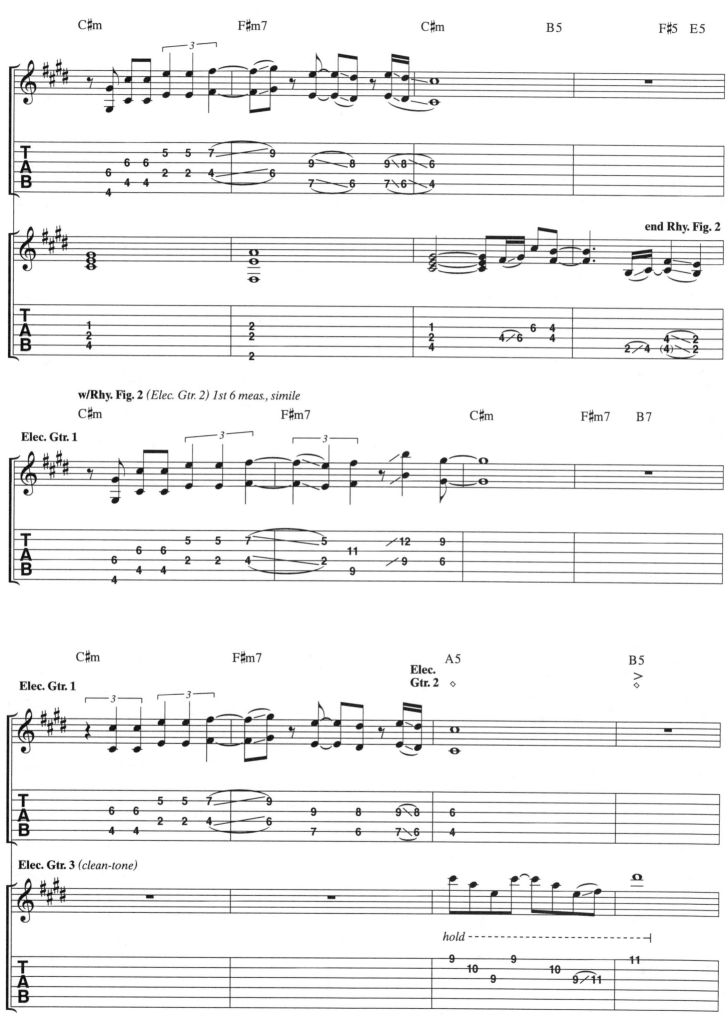

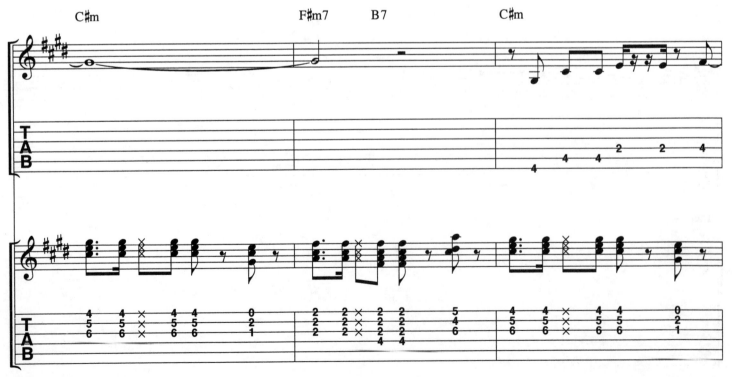

*Composite arrangement.

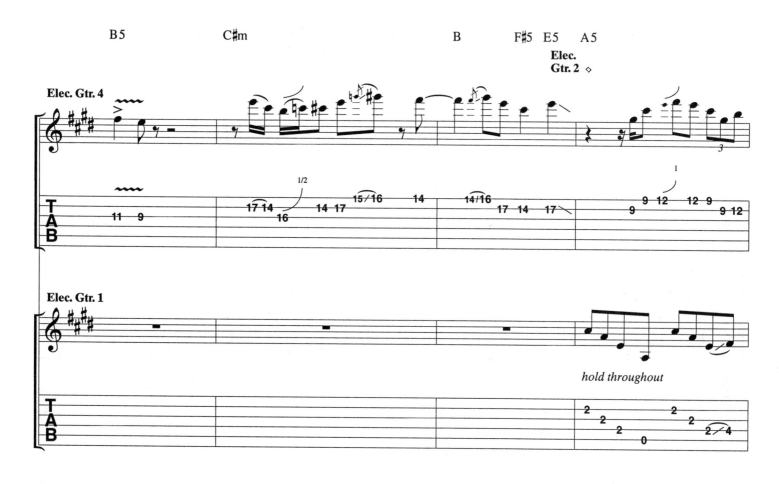

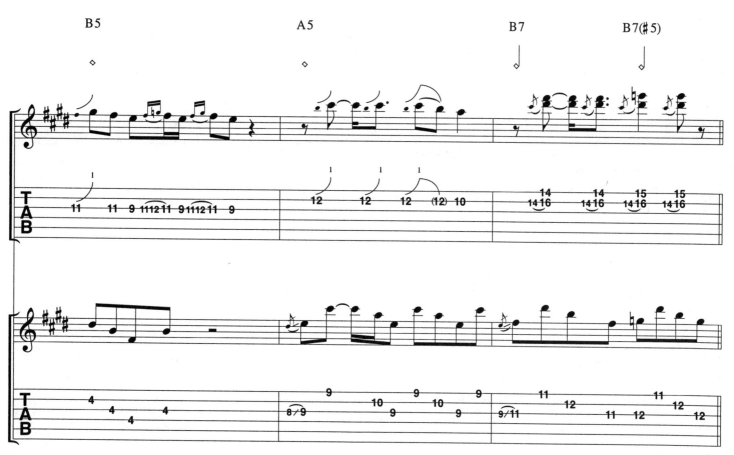

Sway a Little - 17 - 9
PGM0412

w/Rhy. Fig. 2 (*Elec. Gtr 2.*) *1st 6 meas., simile*

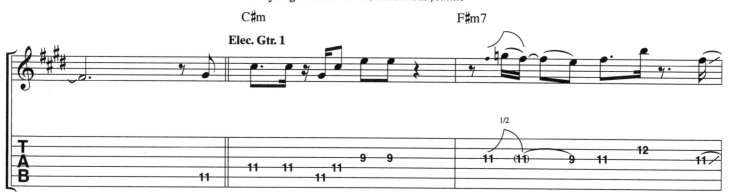

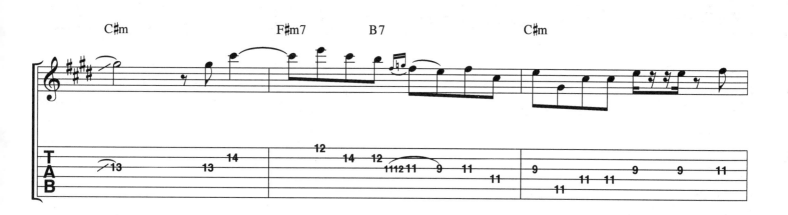

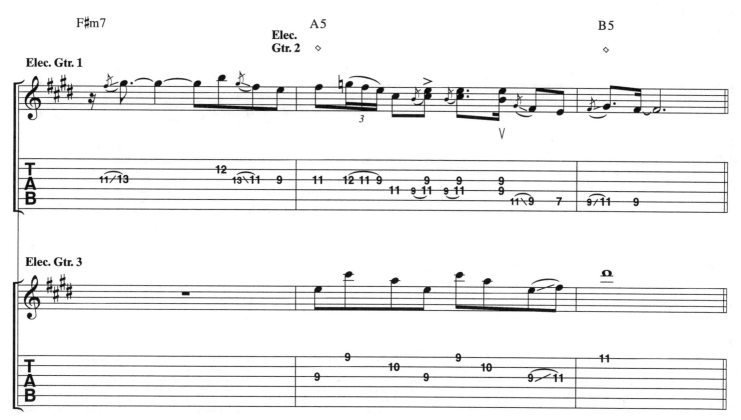

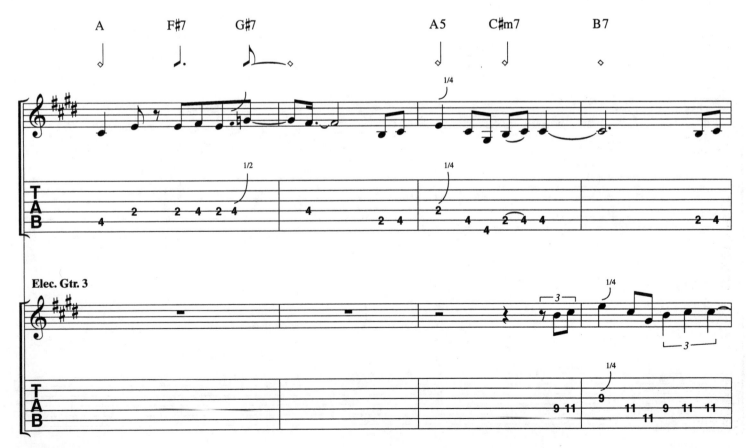

Sway a Little - 17 - 13
PGM0412

100

Guitar Solo:

w/Rhy. Fig. 1 *(Elec. Gtr. 1) 10 1/2 times, simile*

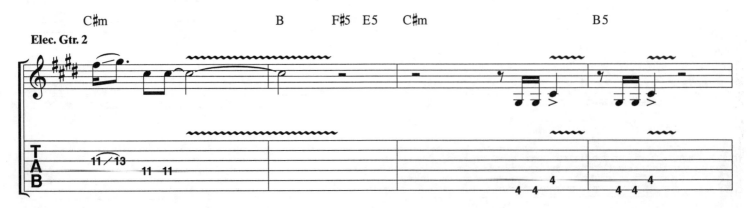

Sway a Little - 17 - 14
PGM0412

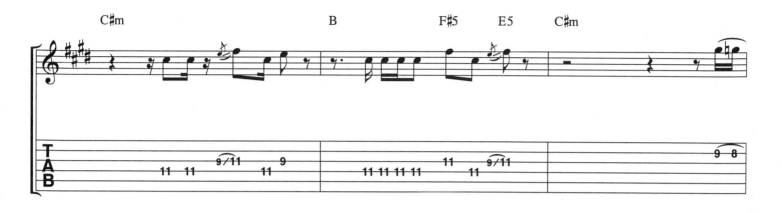

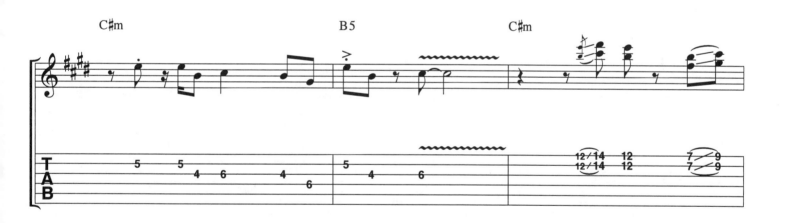

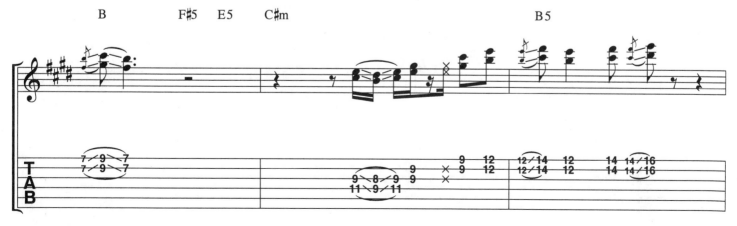

Sway a Little - 17 - 15
PGM0412

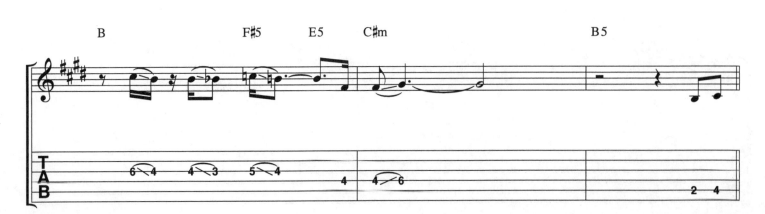

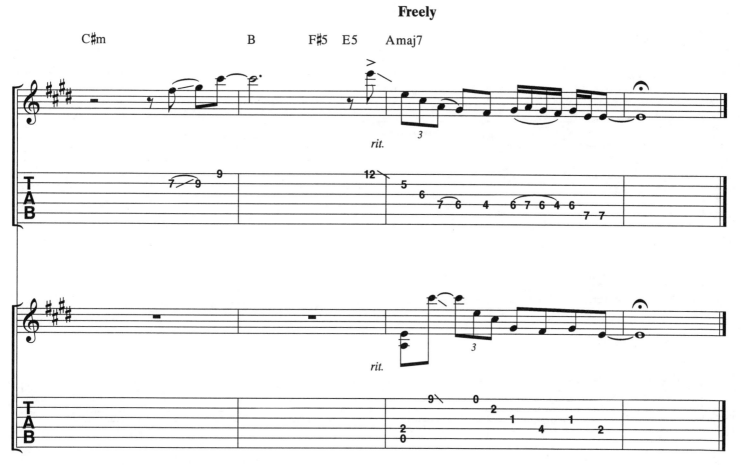

STIMULATION

By JOHNNY A.

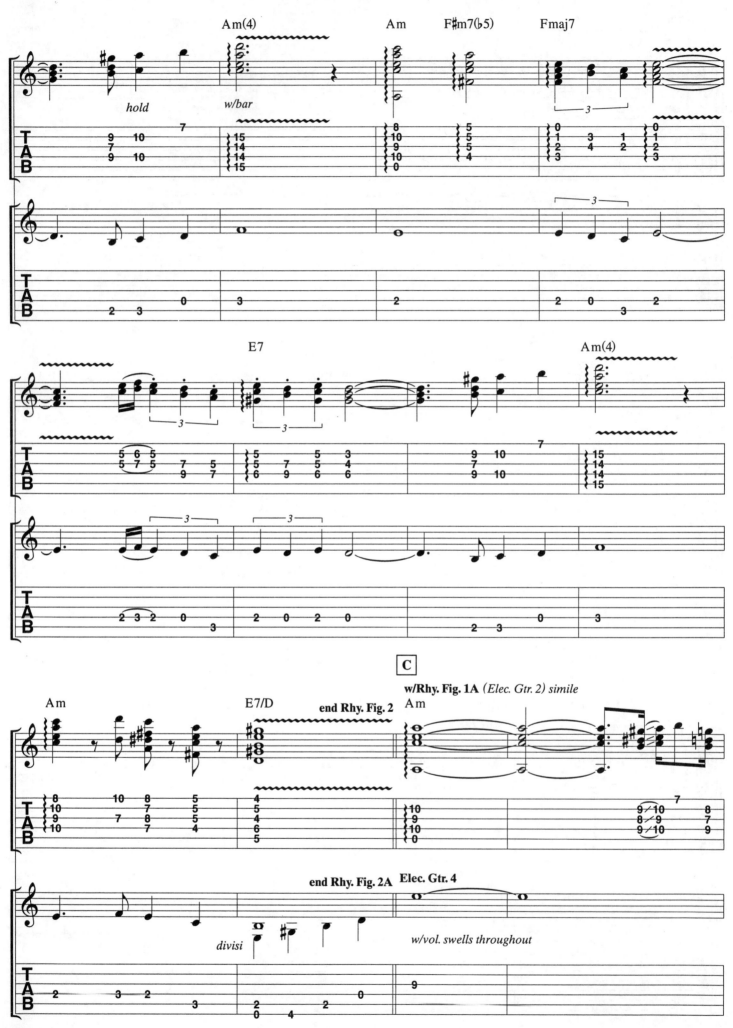

*Notation/tablature reflect capoed gtr.

Guitar Solo:

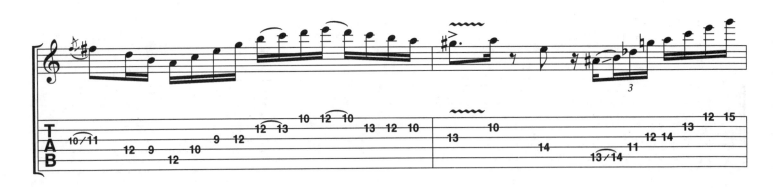

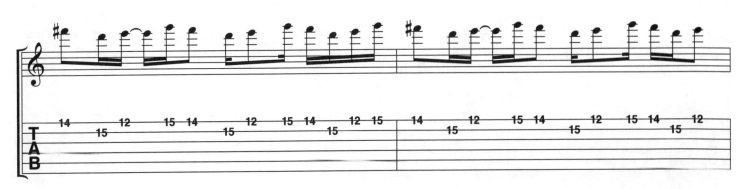

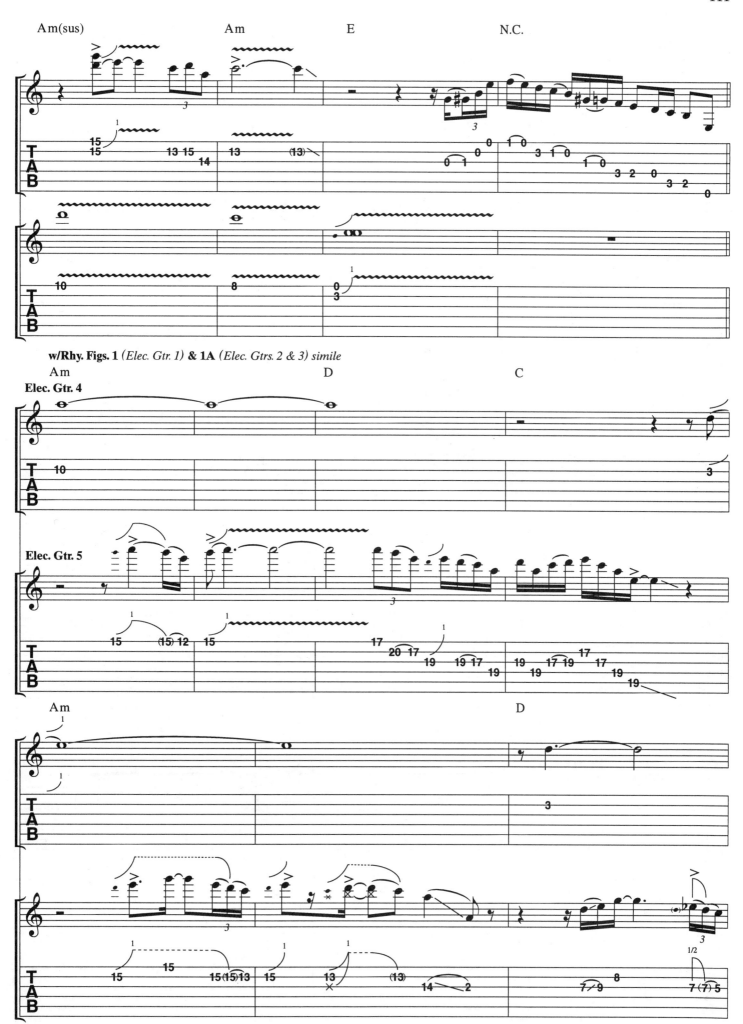

w/Rhy. **Figs. 1** (*Elec. Gtr. 1*) **& 1A** (*Elec. Gtrs. 2 & 3*) *simile*

ANOTHER LIFE

By JOHNNY A.

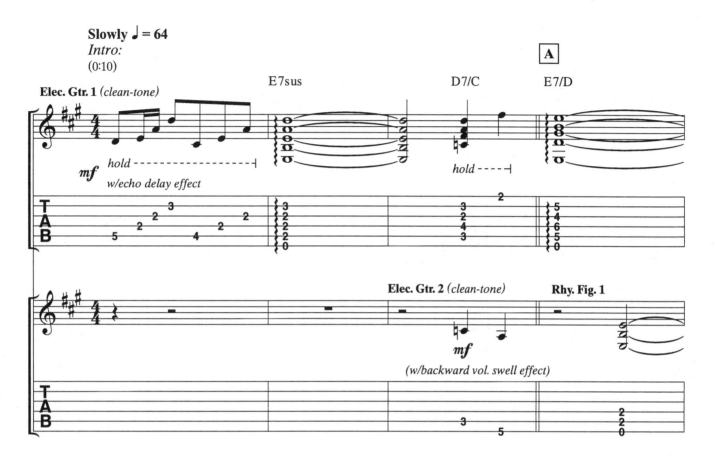

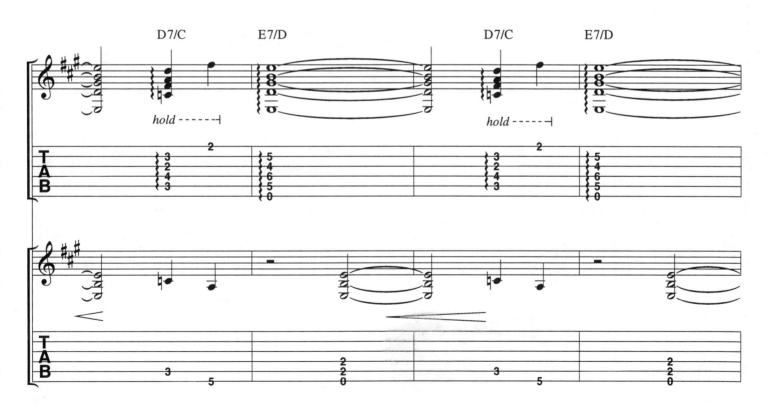

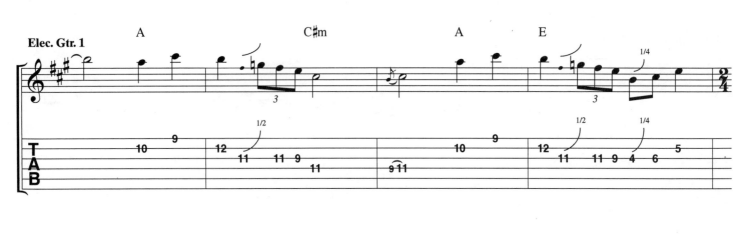

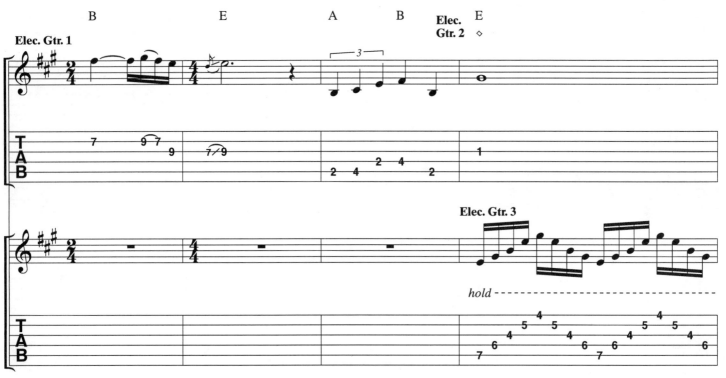

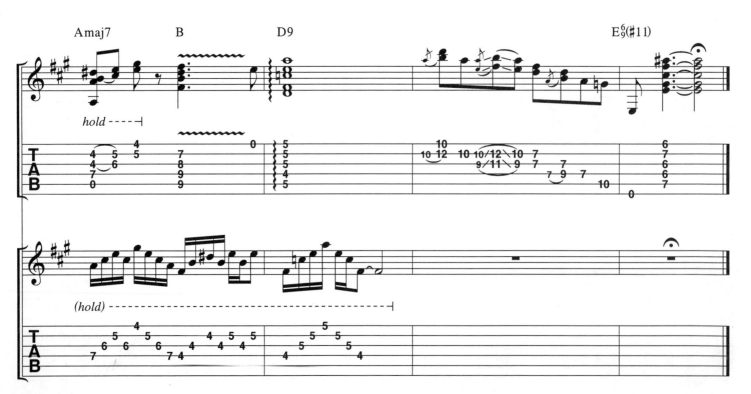

GUITAR TAB GLOSSARY **

TABLATURE EXPLANATION

READING TABLATURE: Tablature illustrates the six strings of the guitar. Notes and chords are indicated by the placement of fret numbers on a given string(s).

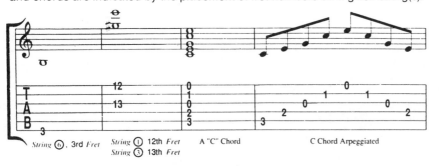

String ⑥, 3rd Fret   String ① 12th Fret   A "C" Chord   C Chord Arpeggiated
String ③ 13th Fret

BENDING NOTES

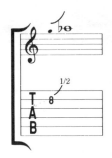

HALF STEP: Play the note and bend string one half step.*

WHOLE STEP: Play the note and bend string one whole step.

PREBEND AND RELEASE: Bend the string, play it, then release to the original note.

RHYTHM SLASHES

STRUM INDICATIONS: Strum with indicated rhythm.

The chord voicings are found on the first page of the transcription underneath the song title.

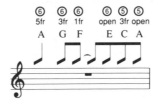

INDICATING SINGLE NOTES USING RHYTHM SLASHES: Very often single notes are incorporated into a rhythm part. The note name is indicated above the rhythm slash with a fret number and a string indication.

*A half step is the smallest interval in Western music; it is equal to one fret. A whole step equals two frets.

**By Kenn Chipkin and Aaron Stang

ARTICULATIONS

HAMMER ON: Play lower note, then "hammer on" to higher note with another finger. Only the first note is attacked.

PULL OFF: Play higher note, then "pull off" to lower note with another finger. Only the first note is attacked.

LEGATO SLIDE: Play note and slide to the following note. (Only first note is attacked).

PALM MUTE: The note or notes are muted by the palm of the pick hand by lightly touching the string(s) near the bridge.

ACCENT: Notes or chords are to be played with added emphasis.

DOWN STROKES AND UPSTROKES: Notes or chords are to be played with either a downstroke (⊓·) or upstroke (∨) of the pick.

© 1990 Beam Me Up Music
c/o CPP/Belwin, Inc. Miami, Florida 33014
International Copyright Secured   Made in U.S.A.   All Rights Reserved

CUSTOM · ART
Gibson
Since 1894
· HISTORIC ·

The Johnny A. Signature Model Gibson Guitar

The new Johnny A. Signature model from the Custom Shop combines several innovative new design aspects with loads of vintage Gibson appointments to create what will surely become a modern classic.

The completely hollow body—with a solid, AAA maple top and tonally carved back and sides—features a contoured outer surface but a flat inner back, resulting in a guitar that resonates more like a flattop than an archtop. An exclusive body style and size, a custom neck profile, and custom pearl fingerboard inlays combine with traditional Gibson features like multi-ply binding, gold hardware, and an ebony fretboard to create an instrument that captures the magic of Gibson's past while eagerly anticipating the future.

See it at www.gibsoncustom.com.